Sandra Markle

Waiting for Ice

Illustrated by
Alan Marks

ᵢⁿᵢ Charlesbridge

With love for Nancy Farrell—S. M.

To Samuel and Jacob, my great nephews—A. M.

Acknowledgments

Sandra Markle would like to thank Dr. Nikita Ovsyanikov, deputy
director of the Wrangel Island State Nature Reserve and senior research
scientist for Institute of Problems of Ecology and Evolution, Russian
Academy of Sciences, for sharing his enthusiasm and expertise.
A special thank-you to Skip Jeffery for his loving support throughout
the creative process.

Published by Charlesbridge
85 Main Street
Watertown, MA 02472
(617) 926-0329
www.charlesbridge.com

Library of Congress Cataloging-in-Publication Data
Markle, Sandra.
    Waiting for ice / by Sandra Markle ; illustrated by Alan Marks.
      p. cm.
    ISBN 978-1-58089-255-1 (reinforced for library use)
    ISBN 978-1-60734-086-7 (ebook pdf)
1. Polar bear—Juvenile literature. 2. Polar bear—Effect of global warming on—Juvenile literature.
[1. Polar bear. 2. Polar bear—Effect of global warming on.] I. Marks, Alan, 1957–
II. Title.
QL737.C27M3455 2012
599.786'1722—dc22   2011002113

Printed in China
(hc) 10 9 8 7 6 5 4 3 2

Illustrations done in watercolor and pencil on Fabriano 5 paper
Display type and text type set in Elroy and Fairfield
Color separations by KHL Chroma Graphics, Singapore
Printed by Jade Productions in Heyuan, Guangdong, China
Production supervision by Brian G. Walker
Designed by Martha MacLeod Sikkema

A polar bear cub, barely ten months old,
leaps out of the waves onto the gravel beach.
She shakes the sea off and looks around.
There are lots of other polar bears on this spit of land.
But she doesn't see her mother.

Screaming, the young cub searches
in one direction, then another.
She sees lots of adult females—
but none is her mother.
The cub runs away, screaming even louder.
Whether orphaned or lost,
the cub is among strangers—
most much bigger than she is.

It's early October. The polar bears have spent the summer
on Wrangel Island, far north of Russia
in the Arctic Ocean, trapped
because the drifting pack ice they roam has melted.
They must wait for the patchwork quilt of ice
to return, so they can hunt for seals and whales
from these floating life rafts.

But this summer has been warmer than usual.
The polar bears crowd together
on a spit of land stretching out into the sea and wait
for the ice that is late in coming.
The young cub roams among them,
searching for her mother.

When another female with a cub blocks her way and growls,
the young cub bolts from the spit, heading inland.
She runs over rock-studded, ice-crusted tundra up a steep slope.
This past December, on another hillside, she was born in a snow den.
Her mother kept her close, safe, and well fed,
even after she climbed out of the den in early April.
Polar bear cubs usually stay with their mothers two to three years.
But this cub is already alone—on her own.

Slowing to a walk, the cub crosses a ridge.
She stops from time to time to lift her head and sniff.
Nearby are jagged cliffs, where all summer
thousands of black-legged kittiwakes nested, raising chicks.
The flock has flown south, but the cub follows her keen nose
and finds a dead bird.
She feeds on this and then walks on,
carrying what's left for later.

After a while the cub curls up
and naps with her back to the wind.
Some signal alerts her—a scent or a sound—
and she opens her eyes to an Arctic fox sneaking up close.

She chases this prey.
But with bushy tail flying, the fox sprints away.
And by the time the cub returns, the fox has circled back
and stolen what was left of the bird.

Several days later, hunger
drives the cub back to the beach.
Now even more polar bears wait on the spit.
There's ice offshore,
but it's the size of giant lily pads
and pancake-thin—too weak to support polar bears.

With the migrating prey gone, the hunters are hungry.
They chew on old whale bones
and fight for the few fish that wash ashore.

Day after day, for nearly two weeks, the cub grabs
a mouthful of food wherever she can.
Most young orphaned cubs die of hunger
or become prey themselves.
Though she grows thin,
this young female stays alive.

The cub is napping on a rise
when the walruses arrive
to rest on the beach.
She awakes to loud barks
and the sight of boulder-sized bodies
resting so close together
that each leans its long tusks on its neighbor.

Hungry polar bears patrol the walrus herd,
on the lookout for the weak or the wounded.
Suddenly, one big male polar bear charges in.

Pushing, grunting walruses stampede into the sea.
A calf lags behind.
The big male bites the calf's neck and pulls it away.
The mother walrus turns with tusks raised to strike.
But the male is already hauling the calf up the rise.
The hungry cub leaps up and trails after him.

When she catches up, the big male stands
with blood-stained face between her and his meal.
She circles and then belly-crawls closer while he feeds.
When she finally takes a bite of the walrus flesh,
the big male growls but lets her stay.

While the cub eats her fill, the snow begins.
By the time the male plods away,
the air is full of swirling flakes.
The cub finds shelter nearby among rocks
and curls up to wait out the storm
roaring ashore from the sea.

For nearly a week, the blizzard rages
while the cub lives on leftovers and sleeps.
When it stops, the whole world is changed.
Pregnant female polar bears head for the mountains
to den in drifts where they'll sleep, give birth,
and keep their cubs safe until spring comes again.
Along the shore is the biggest change of all.
The pack ice is back!

The waiting is over.

Free to roam and hunt, big adult males leave at once.

Over the next few days, young adults follow.

So do mothers with cubs trailing behind them.

The orphaned cub lingers on this land that is

harsh, hungry—and home.

Daily, though, she goes out onto the ice to explore.

One day she stays to nap.
While she sleeps, the ice cracks.
When she awakes,
she's adrift.
Though Wrangel Island is only a short swim away,
she stays.

To grow up, she'll have to learn to hunt
on the Arctic Ocean using ice floes as resting places.
And that is exactly what she will do.
With a leap to another floe,
she heads out onto the ice.

Author's Note

This book is based on the true story of a polar bear nicknamed Tuff. Researcher Dr. Nikita Ovsyanikov, who has spent seventeen years studying polar bears on Wrangel Island, first reported seeing this orphaned cub in October 2002. He didn't hold much hope for her. As a cub-of-the-year, born the previous December or January, she lacked her mother's care and training in hunting and survival. To his amazement, however, the cub did survive, so he gave her the nickname Tuff. He was still convinced, though, that without a mother, she'd never live through her first winter hunting on the Arctic's frozen waters.

This book ends as the cub faces that challenge of winter survival. But Dr. Ovsyanikov reports that the following spring, when the polar bears returned to Wrangel Island, he saw the real Tuff again. Although she was now older and bigger, he had spent so many hours observing her that he easily recognized her. Dr. Ovsyanikov was delighted that Tuff proved she was capable of beating the odds.

Polar Bears Are Amazing!

※ Polar bears are the largest land carnivores, or meat-eating hunters. Males grow to be bigger than females and may be eight to ten feet (2.4 to 3 meters) long. One of the heaviest adult males ever recorded weighed 2,209 pounds (1,002 kilograms).

※ A polar bear's coat is double thick, with long guard hairs over short woolly hairs. Its coat looks white, but its hairs are really hollow and transparent. Any available sunlight easily passes through to its black skin—and black is the perfect color for soaking up heat energy.

※ Polar bears have a layer of blubber, or fat, as much as four and a half inches (11.4 centimeters) thick under their skin. This shields them from the cold and traps their body heat.

Global Warming

The gradual warming of the earth's climate is one of the biggest threats to polar bears. While searching for prey, these predators may swim sixty miles (96 kilometers) without stopping. But they can't swim indefinitely: they need to rest on ice floes in the sea. By mid-July, during the Arctic summer, much of the ocean's ice covering melts or breaks up and drifts far north, forcing polar bears ashore. Many take refuge on Wrangel Island, north of Russia, near their summer hunting grounds. Wrangel Island is far away from other islands and the mainland, so the bears remain trapped there, waiting for ice to surround the island again. Normally, that happens in September. But temperature increases from global climate change mean that the sea now frequently remains free from pack ice for many more weeks—sometimes until late November. Because the island's food supply is primarily migrating birds and walruses, competition for food becomes intense.

Discover More

How Global Warming Works
http://science.howstuffworks.com/global-warming.htm
Discover what's causing global warming and how it effects the earth.
Don't miss the video clip featuring polar bears on Wrangel Island.

Markle, Sandra. *Animal Predators: Polar Bears.* Minneapolis: Lerner,
2004. Follow these top Arctic predators as they hunt, mate, and raise
their young.

Patent, Dorothy Hinshaw. *A Polar Bear Biologist at Work* (Wildlife
Conservation Society Books). New York: Franklin Watts, 2001.
Investigate polar bears with researcher Chuck Jonkel.

Polar Bears International: Bear Facts
http://www.polarbearsinternational.org/bear-facts/
Explore this site's many polar bear facts and photos.

Thornhill, Jan. *This Is My Planet: The Kids' Guide to Global Warming.*
Toronto, Ontario, Canada: Maple Tree Press, 2007.
Explore how the earth can bounce back from this environmental
problem and what you can do to help.